Navigating the Corporate Jungle

How to Avoid Getting Bitten, Poisoned, or Worse

By Scott Rancor

Contents

Foreword

This book is dedicated to the unsung heroes of corporate America. This goes out to all of the analysts, accountants, technical support, human resources, and administrative staff that never get the respect they deserve. They are expected to care and feed for all of the creatures in the corporate jungle while avoiding the natural disasters that prevent them from completing their work as they struggle to survive. I've tried to infuse some humor into this book. Sometimes, in the situations described, humor is the only thing that keeps you going. I hope that this book helps you survive, and maybe even thrive, in the corporate jungle. As we tour this dangerous jungle, for your own safety, please keep your heads and arms inside the vehicle at all times.

- Scott Rancor (2014)

Chapter 1

Natural Disasters – Identifying and Escaping the Natural Perils

For anyone that has worked in corporate America for a substantial period of time, the comparison of this dangerous world to a jungle is not a gargantuan stretch. These environments have a significant number of commonalities. A jungle has hazards that are nature based such as poisonous plants, quick sand, and natural disasters like floods, fires, and storms. Companies large and small have these same challenges. There is the quicksand of the never ending project that, once one enters, they may sink in and never be heard from again. There are the floods of work that come from promised products that have been oversold by eager salesmen that pick up speed and sweep away anyone in their path as the work flows downhill. Fires and storms are much like mergers and acquisitions. They hit violently, leave a great deal of devastation, and require much rebuilding once the bodies have been cleared.

Apart from the perils of the natural world, jungles also have creatures that are scary and dangerous. They can kill, maim, or poison you without little warning. It seems obvious that corporations have these creatures lurking about as well. Just as the Lion pounces upon the unsuspecting gazelle, the manager can pounce upon unsuspecting employees leaving the carnage of mangled carcasses in his or her wake.

This book will continue this either annoying or funny (depending on your opinion) comparison of the jungle and corporate world and will help you navigate through the treacherous corporate path and survive.

Quicksand

In the jungle, quicksand is a mixture of sand, clay, and water. It can appear to be solid ground until some event causes it to become liquefied. It will then suck objects down to a depth where the density of the object is equal to the weight of the displaced mixture.

When a living creature encounters quicksand, it can be harmless if the creature does not panic and simply floats to the top. Once flailing and panic set in, the results can be fatal.

Let's equate this to that mysterious project over in Finance or Human Resources. It may have started with one or two people. As the project progresses and more resources are 'floated' into it, it reaches saturation. Some shocking event, however, can cause it to turn into corporate quicksand. Maybe the CFO actually notices that the project is costing money and needs to be wrapped up. Maybe it gets mentioned to the CEO on the back nine or during the corporate Pilates class. Whatever the event, the project can quickly turn into a viscous pool of resource sucking quicksand. Other resources (people, money, etc.) are thrown into it and as they flail about trying to finish the project, they are sucked deeper and deeper, never to be seen again.

This book is not long enough to detail a strategy for companies to avoid quicksand projects. Besides, this book is not for the mysterious C-Suite executives or even their closely held minions. It is for the poor Joe Schmuck that tends to fall prey to these types of projects. Someone has decided that you would be useful to bring the project to closure so you are thrown in on top of all of the other sunken resources. How do you survive without sinking into the depths with everyone else? Here are some tips that may help:

- **Don't panic and flail about**. What this means is that you have to accept where you are and that you should not take drastic measures to try to escape. Accept that you are on the project but take measures to avoid being sucked so deeply into it that your very survival is threatened. You can do this by looking for the signs that are around you. Look at the history of the project. Have tasks within it been turning in circles where the same mistakes are being repeated? Are others that have been on the project for a while simply showing up and performing these tasks without an eye toward an eventual end? If you see these signs in a quicksand project, look for ways to avoid the circular tasks and focus on the ones with definitive beginnings and endings.

- **Reach for a branch or a vine.** If learned nothing else from the episodes of Gilligan's Island and the Tarzan movies that I watched as a kid, you can get out of quicksand by grabbing a branch or a vine. These lifesaving objects may be close at hand if you look for them or they may require someone else extending them to you so that you can make your escape. If you find yourself in a quicksand project, you should always be looking for a lifesaving limb that you can grab and pull yourself to safety. Maybe that limb is another position in the company in another division. It might even be another job. You should keep in mind that corporate quicksand differs from the jungle variety. The sand, clay, and water mixture is easily washed away from your clothes in nature. In the corporate world, the stains from a quicksand project will be permanently imprinted on you if you do not escape before the survivors are collected.

Floods

I have done my share of time working for technology companies. Technology companies like IBM, Microsoft, and others have sales people that are savvy and knowledgeable of the company's product line. Smaller technology companies, not so much. The guy who is selling contract management software today may have been selling used Hyundai automobiles yesterday. They listen to the features that the customer wants, they tell the customer the price, the customer complains about the price, they have a mythical conversation with a mythical supervisor over the customer's demands, and then they return and tell all who will listen that they fought for the customer to give them what they want. They do some fancy paperwork that is only read by the legal department, a fearsome dark corner of the jungle that we will talk about later, and then the deal is done. In a small technology company where account management is a foreign concept, the contact between the sales person and the customer is now concluded forever and the paperwork is thrown over the wall to the technical staff that must make good on what was promised during the sales negotiations.

Now the flood begins. From high atop Sales Mountain, the flood starts with a trickle. Salespeople have promised the customer the world and the oceans of that world have started to gather and flow down toward those that are performing the actual work. A delivery date has likely been promised and the velocity of the waters from those collective oceans will flow toward the technical team and wash them away if they cannot stem the flow and complete the work as promised. The water is much too swift to be dammed up. Many damns, however, and other choice words will flow back uphill toward the sales team but will go unheard in the roar of the flood because in the corporate world, nothing flows uphill.

Fires and Storms

In a forest or a jungle, fires can be started by storms. A well placed lightning strike can set a large area ablaze which can lead to massive damage. A fire can also be started by a careless idiot with little regard for the environment that perhaps starts a fire too close to the trees or doesn't ensure that his or her fire has been extinguished satisfactorily.

Mergers and acquisitions within a company can be compared to these devastating events. Having been through a number of these activities, I can say that your best defense might be to spray water on your own house and hope that the fire passes you by. Mergers can be painful. Think of two adults in their late 30s or early 40s deciding they are in love and that they want to move in together. They both have their own stuff. They may have their own friends. They have their finances separated, and they are each set in their own ways. When two companies merge, it can be a similar situation, only worse. Imagine that the two lovebirds have to decide what stuff to keep and then sell the other stuff in a garage sale. Then, they have to go through their friends and decide which ones they are going to keep and who is getting kicked to the curb. Finally, they are going to go over each other's bank statements with severe scrutiny and argue over who is worth more. This is not the way to start a loving relationship. In the corporate world, the merger or acquisition process can put two companies that come together to be a 'blended family' in this same awkward state. The relationship starts out with a tension that is hard to erase as the new entity begins to do business.

What does this mean to Ms. Schmuck who works in Payroll or Technical Support? It means that, no matter what your level, you should do your homework. This can be tricky because information is held very confidential during these types of proceedings as to not sour the deal. The trick is knowing what confidential means in a typical company. It means listen to the rumors. In all of my years in corporate America, rumors have a very high accuracy rate. They usually come from highly placed people or those that feed and care for them. They have this juicy information and can't resist telling someone about it. Listen to those rumors. They're usually true to a high degree.

The rumors will tell you who the players are. If your company, Acme, is merging with American Widgets, go on to the other company's web site and find out whom their leadership is. Did the CEO and CFO of American Widgets go to the same college? Are they from the same city? If so, they may be buddies meaning that the CFO of Acme should not buy green bananas. If the CFO looks older than the Crypt Keeper, then your guy might survive and, if you are in his department, this news might be somewhat good. I say somewhat, because, like in any storm, one well-placed lightning strike or tornado touchdown can be a game changer. No one is 100% safe in these scenarios until well after the deal is finalized. The first step that you should take when your company faces merger or acquisition is UPDATE YOUR RESUME!

Droughts

Who has not worked for a company where there was some kind of hiring freeze or expense cutback? I once worked for a client as a consultant that wanted to demonstrate belt-tightening in the face of bad financial performance. They did this by cutting back on office supplies. No pens, paper clips, computer paper, or any other office doodad could be purchased without the CEO's signature. This was an organization with over 20,000 employees. To further help them figure out how to turnaround their financial woes, they hired a big four consulting company to come in and look at their books and tell them where to slash and burn. As I sat around the table in an executive meeting watching the CEO search for a pen to use, I did a quick tally of the $700 per hour consultants sitting in the room for that hour. Let's just say that many pens could have been purchased instead.

Why do these droughts occur in the corporate jungle? If the company is public, it's part of the quest to do anything to improve the bottom line and meet earnings projections for investors. If earnings aren't met, dividends aren't paid, and investors don't invest. If the company is private, they may be trying to make sure that this week's payroll checks don't bounce. I once worked for a company with a CEO that was so benevolent that the staff agreed to work for a period of time for no pay just so that the company would not go under. Ah, the good old days.

It is important to be able to recognize the drought periods for what they are. Are they an image enhancer as in public companies? If they are multiple and building, this points to something more serious. A failing company is one that you want to escape from quickly. There is no glory in going down with the ship. In fact, the captain of your corporate ship, the CEO, may be the first rat to leave. Wow, now I've gone from jungles to ships at sea. Oh well. It works. The bottom line is recognizing a temporary drought and differentiating it from a Great Depression era dustbowl.

Avalanches

So you're probably wondering why an avalanche is listed as a natural disaster that occurs in a jungle. For the purpose of this book (and so I can use the avalanche metaphor) our jungle has a mountain range next to it that is prone to avalanches. Now that you've made that leap of faith, let's talk about corporate avalanches. What are they? How do they happen? Can they be prevented? How does one survive?

An avalanche in nature occurs spontaneously during storms. We talked about storms earlier. So some corporate storms can result in avalanches where everything collapses at once and all you can do is get out of the way. An avalanche in nature is associated with snowpack that fails when the load becomes too much to be supported. In the corporate world, a large project or initiative can also lose support when the load on resources becomes too large. Like a yodeler in the Alps that can trigger the snow to cascade down (I watch too many cartoons), some well-placed comments in an executive meeting can cause an avalanche. Once a CFO, or worker, a Project Management Office (PMO) mentions that a project is consuming too many resources too fast, executives feel compelled to jump into action and take control of the situation by either accelerating the work or pulling the plug. Accelerating the work can result in the corporate avalanche. Work accelerates at a pace that corners are cut and fundamental processes are shortened resulting in the underlying support or methodology of the project to crumble. Projects that are accelerated in this way rarely succeed and, like a snowy avalanche, wreak havoc on everything in their path. The resources involved in these projects are often buried and, if they survive, are afraid to venture onto mountainous projects again.

How can these corporate avalanches be prevented? In nature, towns and ski resorts that are prone to avalanches often set off controlled explosions around areas of building snow to lessen the strain on the supporting snow underneath. So how does this translate to our corporate example? If a large project is consuming a large number of resources, there may be other small peripheral projects that can be 'blown up' to free up resources to feed the large project before it turns into an avalanche. The important thing to remember is to move out of the path of one of these projects if the avalanche is inevitable.

Earthquakes

An earthquake is caused by a sudden release of energy in the Earth's crust. I remember the first time I experienced and earthquake. I was in Northern California and had been to a cocktail party where I had sampled a few too many cocktails. I was pleasantly sedated and went back to my hotel room to sleep it off before a full day of meetings the next day. At about 4 AM the room started to shake for about 20 seconds. After I swore off drinking forever, I realized where I was and what had happened. It was a minor tremor (major to me) and there was no aftershock or further shaking for the remainder of my trip.

In looking at the corporate world, there are different degrees of earthquakes that take place within organizations. The sudden departure of a key employee can register as a tremor, or, if his or her vision was driving the organization, it might be a major shakeup with several aftershocks. If an organization is built in a solid fashion, it will survive. If it is not, or didn't plan properly for the earthquake that the departure of a key person can bring, it may crumble. Apple is a prime example of this. The company nearly collapsed after the involuntary departure of Steve Jobs. It could be argued that the company's current status atop the consumer technology organizations is due directly to Jobs' return as CEO. He brought with him the ideas for the i-pod, i-phone, i-pad, and i-tunes. With his death and the loss of those innovative ideas from his mind, it will be interesting to see where Apple is when the life cycles for these products expire. The last few updates since Jobs passed away seem to consist of changing the size of the existing products or copying the innovations made by others.

Earthquakes can be caused by the arrival of a new key person in an organization. When J.C. Penney brought on Ron Johnson as CEO straight from his successes at Target and with the

Apple Store chain, they expected him to reinvigorate their old-school company. Johnson came in and made some fatal mistakes that those who have experienced multiple successes often make. First, he believed he couldn't fail. Second, he didn't respect J.C. Penney's customer base and traditions. By ending a long-standing tradition, customer coupons he alienated customers. By not testing this new approach and implementing it abruptly, Johnson caused an earthquake and was swallowed up in the damage. He was out as CEO after only 17 months. Because J.C. Penney was so damaged by Johnson's tactics, its recovery is still in doubt.

Chapter 2

Beware of the Beasts

We've identified the natural disasters that can influence our corporate jungle. What about the creatures lurking about? Jungles have many varieties of creatures from the ferocious predators to the loathsome scavengers, and all the way down to the innocent prey. How do these creatures relate to corporate America? You will be surprised at the similarities. Put on your pith helmet and allow me to be your guide as we observe and comment on the corporate beasts in their natural habitat.

The Predators

A predator is known as one animal that feeds on another. When a python swallows a rodent whole or a lion tracks down a weak antelope and feeds on its raw flesh, which is predatory behavior. When an executive extracts as much knowledge and work from a subordinate as possible and then uses that knowledge and the output of the work to enhance their own position, this is also predatory behavior. There are different types of predators in the natural and corporate jungle. Predators can ambush their prey like a lion or cheetah seeking out the weak or young members of a herd. Predators can work together in groups like wolves hunting as a coordinated team. A predator can succeed through brutal strength like a bear. Predators can also catch their prey using speed and agility. A dolphin can plow through a school of fish and swallow multiple fish whole before they know what hit them. A whale, though not usually considered a predator, can strain through countless gallons of water straining out the helpless plankton and devouring them by the thousands.

With the variety of predators that exist, let's take a look at the types of predators that we have in the typical corporate office. We'll start with the scary ones and work our way down the food chain.

The Big Cats

Depending on the jungle and where it's located, the king of the jungle is usually a big cat. It might be a lion, leopard, or tiger, but these predators at the top of the food chain have many things in common, but they also have differences. In a corporation, the king of the jungle may be a CEO, a board chairman, or an owner. Let's look at these different corporate predators and determine their characteristics and, more importantly, how to avoid becoming their prey.

Lions

The big cats; lions, tigers, jaguars, and leopards, are closely related as a species.

Although characterized as the king of the jungle, lions are typically smaller than tigers. Their appearance, however, with their 80's hair band mane makes them the rock star of the big cats. Of all the feline predators, lions are the most social. They form groups known as prides. They actually prefer to scavenge food, but when they do hunt, it is usually the lioness that hunts while the males of the pride stay back and watch the young.

This type of behavior corresponds to the lion-like CEO that exists in traditional companies. They lord over their organization from a corner office delegating their hunting to others. They scavenge from the work of others. CEOs of this genus usually have a lioness (administrative assistant) that does their hunting for them securing everything from coffee to travel arrangements and organization of their calendar.

Tigers

In contrast to the lion, the tiger is the largest of the predatory cat species. Tigers are an endangered species in the wild as well as in corporations. Unlike the lion, adult tigers are loners and establish distinct territories. Tigers do most of their own hunting and prey on large and medium-sized animals. They've even been known to prey on other smaller predators.

In the corporate jungle, the tiger is like the entrepreneurial CEO that is hungry to grow his organization (territory). This type of CEO lives by merger and acquisition, swallowing up other organizations and their leaders along the way. This type of CEO, while not endangered, is much rarer than the typical CEO that seeks moderate growth and thrives on the status quo.

Fast Cats

The third class of big cats in our jungle includes those that relay on speed and brutality to subdue their prey. While smaller in size, these cats can be much more effective and ferocious. Included in this group are the leopards, jaguars, cougars, cheetahs, and other similar cats. Like the tigers, these cats are solitary and territorial with males having larger territories than females. When it comes to hunting, these cats are extremely strong and agile. They often carry prey that approaches twice their own weight high up into trees to hide their prize and feed their young. While tigers have a healthy respect for each other's territory, these smaller cats have been known to aggressively fight with each other in disputes over their areas.

Let's look for this type of predator in the corporate jungle. This type of CEO is more entrepreneurial than his or her lion or tiger-like peers. They are agile, moving from company to company as the opportunity arises. They often do what it takes to achieve their goals even if the method or outcome is not popular, or in some cases, 100% legal. I look at Bill Gates when I think of this type of CEO. It can be argued that Microsoft was founded on a predatory event. MS-DOS was the operating system that put Microsoft on the map. Bill Gates hired a programmer, Tim Paterson, in 1981 and bought DOS 1.10 for $75,000. Gates then renamed it to MS-DOS and licensed it to IBM for a hefty profit. Paterson never got a penny above the original $75,000. Gates was more agile than his competitors in recognizing the value of this product and snapping it up before they could. He made it his own just as he has with Windows (originally developed by Xerox) and many other products that Microsoft has gobbled up over the years.

Bears and Wolves

Bears and wolves are animals that can exist in the jungle depending on where in the world it exists. Though these animals are being mentioned together, they are dissimilar in behavior in both the natural and corporate world. Bears are big lumbering animals. They are viewed as cute and stuffed representations of them have been comforting children for decades. This is all true until you corner or poke them. Then you will discover the powerful claws and teeth that can easily end your existence.

Bears

Just as there are various species of Bear, from the cute and cuddly panda to the imposing grizzly, the bears in the corporate jungle vary as well. Let's talk about the most obvious bear in corporate culture, the CFO. Just like a momma bear protecting her cubs, the CFO is fiercely protective of the company's finances and those that manage it. The finance department and their processes is often a mystery to other non-support functions. Just as a bear will protect a carcass, regardless of who it belongs to, the CFO will protect budgets regardless of which department controls it. In my experience, in the unfortunate scenario where the technology department reports to the CFO, the battles can be legendary. The CFO wants expenditures on technology minimized while demanding a higher level of performance than is humanly possible with the paltry budget provided.

Like bears in the wild, the CFO and the entire finance department can go into a period of hibernation where they don't meddle with surrounding departments. These periods usually coincide with audits that seem to take place at regular intervals. During a financial audit, the CFO will be locked away in a room somewhere with mysterious dark-suited consultants from some other jungle. All meetings with the finance department are canceled until the audit concludes. To balance this hibernation period, the CFO will emerge very hungry from an audit, especially if it did not go well, and will devour any unplanned spending requests or departments that have spent more than planned.

Wolves

Any company that has a legal department doesn't need a full-fledged description of wolves in the corporate jungle. Wolves travel in packs. We've heard that often. Lawyers can function on their own, but the danger associated with them increases exponentially as their numbers increase. I have worked in companies where there is a single, in-house legal counsel. My observation of this dynamic is that the legal counsel's job is to disagree with everyone and question how everyone is doing their job. When questioned about how the legal department functions and why things take so long to flow through the legal process, teeth are bared and hackles are raised in defense of the overworked, understaffed nature of the area.

When lawyers gather in packs of the same species, they are virtually invulnerable to any type of attack. They will, however, attack lawyers of other species just as wolves will attack coyotes, foxes, and even other wolves when their spoils (prey) is under dispute. My experience with these corporate wolves results in a recommendation to minimize all contact. Just give them what they want, like the zookeeper throwing raw meat over the fence to captive wolves, any direct contact with the legal department can be dangerous.

Large Animals

In our jungle, the largest animals aren't necessarily the most dangerous unless they are provoked or cornered. This is also true in the corporate jungle. Very often the largest animals are among most intelligent and most experienced, but can also do a great deal of damage when provoked. A rhinoceros, from a distance, looks calm and slow. This is not true when it is charging toward you. Elephants look gentle and comical in the circus, but if you read the book, Water for Elephants, you know that they can turn and wreak havoc quickly and effectively. They are also known for never forgetting. These large and imposing animals have counterparts in the corporate jungle.

Elephants

Elephants have a reputation as a large, benevolent animal known for circus performing and a high degree of intelligence. They are social animals. They not only show a high degree of loyalty to their own group, but also are known to show collaboration with outsiders as well. Communication is extremely important to Elephants. They communicate through touch, sound, and the vibrations they cause on the ground. They are known to exhibit the same sentience and learning abilities as other mammals like apes and dolphins.

All is not just sweetness and light when it comes to the elephant. They can be aggressive against humans. It usually takes some type of perceived threat to cause this behavior although some elephant attacks were traced to drunkenness from consuming fermented fruit. Elephants are an endangered species in the wild and have been poached for the ivory in their tusks.

So where do we find our elephants in the corporate jungle? They are rarely found amongst the highest level executives, yet they are usually more important to the organization then anyone in the "C" suite. Picture the wise old database administrator or the manager in purchasing that has negotiated countless vendor contracts. Their contributions to an organization are often immeasurable. They have a knowledge that transcends departments and administrative teams. They are the go-to person for every strange request and historical recollection in the organization. These individuals are extremely good to know and establish rapport with in an organization. It is equally important to remember not to corner or threaten them (or feed them fermented fruit) or they can stampede and destroy everything in their path. Because of their deep, cross-functional knowledge, they can be both an asset and a threat to an organization if that knowledge is not collected and shared. The worst that can happen is for this knowledge to be taken to the elephant graveyard.

Rhinoceros

Unlike the elephant, the rhinoceros is characterized by a small brain and less than stellar intelligence. They are solidly built with a formidable horn and very poor eyesight. They will attack anything that they view as a threat. The combination of their small brain and their lack of vision, however, makes their judgment as to what represents a threat questionable. When they do attack, they cause significant damage whether the target deserved to be targeted or not.

Can you think of individuals that are like a rhinoceros in the corporate jungle? I can think of many examples. One in particular refers to a company controller that I had the necessity to work with. If this individual viewed a project, department, individual, or piece of equipment as a threat, no mercy was shown. The threat was charged at and often destroyed without good reason just because the narrow vision and bombastic style of this rhino-like controller viewed it as a worthy target. I will not comment on the brain size of this individual, but there may have been a valid comparison to the rhino on this point as well.

The best way to handle the corporate rhinoceros is to avoid it if possible. Do not make eye contact, stay downwind, and whatever you do, don't provoke it. If it does charge at you, try to hide behind something sturdy. If possible, find an elephant to use as a barrier. The corporate rhinoceros can truly be a formidable danger with its combination of a small brain, lack of vision, but incredible ramming power.

Hippopotamus

The mysterious hippopotamus; it spends most of its day hidden in the water. Hippos leave the water as evening approaches to nibble on the grasses within a short distance from the water. They follow the same path every day for their entire lives. They are somewhat territorial and have the lovely practice of spinning their tails while defecating so that their own distinct feces is spread to mark their boundaries. They can be aggressive when they feel their territory is being encroached upon. They will attack and kill crocodiles when they get too close and will even attack boats without apparent provocation.

Now, on to the corporate jungle hippopotamus. These are the individuals that stay under the radar. They stay out of sight and venture out of their office or department only when absolutely necessary. This should not be mistaken for being passive. A passive-aggressive nature, much like the hippo, is the modus operandi for these corporate creatures. They establish their influence, similar to the hippo, by fling their own brand of misinformation (feces) around the organization seeing what will stick (a disgusting metaphor, I must admit). Like the rhinoceros, they are prone to attack without warning. Unlike those horned idiots, however, they know very well where there territory and boundaries are and will remind anyone that comes near without provocation. If you identify a corporate hippo, stay clear of the trajectory of their misinformation. Recognize them for what they are, and avoid becoming like them at all cost. I often find corporate hippos dwelling in places like the legal department (amongst the wolves), in compliance areas, security departments and, of course, in human resources.

Chapter 3

For the Birds

Eagles

Eagles are powerfully built, noble birds that build their nests high atop trees and other lofty perches. Among birds of prey, they are considered the top of the food chain. Eagles have long been symbols in religion and for countries. The bald eagle is the enduring symbol for the United States even though Benjamin Franklin wanted the symbol to be the wild turkey.

Eagles in the corporate world are rare. Lee Iacocca of Ford and, later, Chrysler Corporation, Robert Wright of General Electric, and Steve Jobs of Apple come to mind as leaders that were the symbols of the companies they led. These individuals shaped their companies in their own image and had a great deal of success doing so. It can be argued that leaders like this are bred and not trained to become the people that they are. If you spot an eagle in your company, grab on to their talons and follow them to the top. It may be a bumpy ride, but a strong alliance with corporate eagles will be well worth it.

Falcons

The falcon is the symbol of the United States Air Force. In Star Wars, the most famous ship is Han Solo's Millennium Falcon. Why are falcons recognized in this way? The have incredible speed and maneuverability, which makes them formidable hunters. Falcons also have incredible vision and have scored the highest among birds in terms of intelligence.

In the corporate world, falcons are not as iconic as eagles. The corporate falcons are the leaders that can change directions quickly to get what they want. An example of this type of leader would be Amazon's founder, Jeff Bezos. He founded Amazon in his garage as an online bookstore in 1995. In the less than 20 years since then, Amazon has grown into a powerhouse for online selling of everything from Aardvark Habanero Hot Sauce to Zyrtec. Amazon has also demonstrated the ability to take on other exalted powerhouses in industries like publishing and consumer electronics. Bezos has an incredible vision and the ability to change directions and bring his multi-billion dollar company along for the ride. If you feel like you have the stomach to keep up with a falcon, follow along.

Vultures

Vultures have long been a despised creature in literature and in reality because of the job that they do. They are scavengers. They consume cast off scraps that other animals didn't want or were finished with. They are often viewed as disgusting, but they do perform a vital function in nature by disposing of animal carcasses that might carry disease and other undesirable byproducts of decomposition. They have incredibly strong stomachs and are able to consume meat that would make other animals sick.

Let's think about which corporate figure represents the vulture. When a company goes through a large-scale scandal, it may or may not survive. The corporate vultures come in and clean up the carnage left behind. This may be the disbanding and selling of corporate assets or the cleaning up of the debris that was left behind to make way for restructuring. Unless you like this kind of work, the best advice, if you survive the initial carnage, is to stand back and let the vultures do their work.

Owls

Owls are viewed as the wise, night dwelling denizens in nature. The owls association with wisdom goes back to ancient Greek mythology and has been perpetuated in western culture. The vision and hearing of owls is especially suited to nocturnal behavior. The structure of their bodies and wings allows them to swoop silently out of the darkness to feed on rodents and insects with surgical precision.

Companies can either employee corporate owls or hire them in the guise of consultants. These owls can surgically swoop down and eliminate vermin within an organization. They are usually silent and sometimes nocturnal hanging out in conference rooms with dark suits having secret meetings. Like the owls in nature, they are viewed as wise because their appearance and because of their hefty fees. If you see a gathering of corporate owls in a conference room in your workplace, take cover. You don't want to be noticed.

Parrots

Parrots are the colorful flying members of the jungle. There are many different varieties and sizes, but they do have some things in common. Most of them are very colorful and many have distinct plumage. Some species of parrot are able to mimic the human voice and other sounds quite convincingly. Parrots are desirable because of their appearance and talent for mimicry.

In corporate America, there are parrots in the workplace. These are usually middle management types that are aspiring to be in a higher station. They will imitate what they hear from those in power in order to demonstrate their proximity to them. Very often, they may repeat information based on their own interpretation of it and not with total understanding of what is being said. Parrots usually won't make the transformation to eagles or falcons, it is only in their nature to imitate greatness, not emanate it.

Peacocks

Peacocks, the colorful male of the peafowl species, are mentioned here because of their similarities and differences to parrots. Peacocks are colorful with distinctive tail feathers that are very long. When trying to attract attention or when trying to repel a predator, a peacock will fan its tail feathers and make a very loud noise. It is theorized that the eye-like design on each feather intimidates prey into thinking there are multiple eyes staring them down.

Are there peacocks in the corporate environment? Yes, there are. They similar to the corporate parrot in that they seek to be noticed. These peacocks, however, do not have the conduit to information from leadership. The noise that comes from them is meant to attract attention or intimidate, but usually doesn't have much meaningful information. Corporate Peacocks may pretend that they have a lot of eyes, or allies, but it may just be a smokescreen.

Chapter 4

Primates - Close to Human

Apes are the closest on the evolutionary scale to humans. They can range from the powerful gorilla to the human-like chimpanzees

Gorillas

Gorillas are intelligent, social, and powerful. They are not quite human in the way they carry themselves. They can only travel on two feet for short distances and spend most of their time walking on their rear legs and the knuckles of their hands. They tend to intimidate rather than actually attack and have a series of steps they follow when they are going to charge. They start out with hooting which eventually progresses to chest beating and ends with thumping the ground. Gorillas usually rally around one elder or silverback that will protect the rest of the troop, often at the cost of his own life.

Gorillas in the corporate environment do exist. They are a bit of a throwback to the days when management by intimidation was the rule rather than the exception. Their intimidation tactics are not generally accepted in the modern workplace and, like their primate counterpart, they are a species that faces extinction in today's diverse, politically correct corporate culture.

There may be some limited effectiveness of this type of management in some corporate environments, but, for the most part, they are a vestige of past corporate environments. If you encounter a gorilla, don't make any threatening or sudden movements and do your best to get out of their territory as quickly as possible.

Chimpanzees

The chimpanzee is the closest relative to humans that exist in nature. Chimps can walk upright while carrying objects in their hands. Their reach is very long as their arms are longer than their legs. Their intelligence is very high. They can create tools for gathering food and other purposes. They have sophisticated verbal and nonverbal communication. As they mature, male chimpanzees have been known to be very aggressive, especially when in captivity toward humans. It is not clear if this aggressiveness is an attempt at dominance, or frustration from being controlled for a long period of time. Their considerable strength makes them dangerous when they become aggressive.

Let's think about the characteristics of the chimpanzee in the wild and then relate them to certain corporate citizens. A corporate chimpanzee might equate to someone in middle management that has a good deal of intelligence. They can create tools and innovative processes to facilitate smooth and effective operation within their department. Over time, however, the organization's leadership may determine that this middle-manager has limits to what they can achieve. After a long period of constant frustration from the lack of acceptance by the higher-order primates, these middle managers might become aggressive or spiteful. This can be remedied by facilitating their movement to a new environment. This may include transport to a new job in a different organization.

If you find yourself becoming a chimpanzee, it might be time for a change. There are many reasons that senior leadership in an organization may prevent a middle-manager from reaching that next level. It could be perception, correct or incorrect. It could be what is viewed as a limiting factor. The important thing for someone in this position is to recognize what is causing the perception or limiting factor, overcoming it if possible, or moving to a new organization if it is not. Continuing to let the frustration build will only lead to negative consequences.

Monkeys

Like humans, gorillas, and chimpanzees, monkeys are members of the primate family, but at a much lower level. Although viewed as links in the human evolutionary chain, monkeys do not have the same sophistication as higher order primates. Many species still have prehensile tails that act like an extra limb. Monkeys have had an interesting relationship with humans. They are pets and can even act as service animals for the disabled. On the controversial side, because of their close physiology to humans, they have been used in lab experiments for disease and drug research and have even been sent into space as early cosmonauts and astronauts. Monkeys have been used, and even sacrificed when something is too dangerous for humans.

It seems like we have those employees in organizations that share characteristics with these lower order primates. Think of those entertaining individuals that jump from task to task working happily away. Beware, however, if they are cornered. In the wild, monkeys are known to throw objects at those that threatening them including, unfortunately, their own feces. Think about the corresponding feces-like objects thrown around at the workplace. This would include rumors, flaming emails, comments at meetings and in other group settings, and other potential career-damaging actions.

You might see corporate monkeys staffed on a long drawn-out project with a lot of overtime. The high burnout rate and turnover associated with projects like this is expected and the resources are often viewed as interchangeable. There are positives to gaining experience as a corporate monkey on one of these projects, just don't let yourself become a burnout or, even worse, be permanently be viewed as one of these high-capacity, low-value resources.

Chapter 5

Rodents

Rodents make up about 40% of all mammals. There are many different species ranging from disgusting rats, cute and cuddly bunnies, to industrious beavers. The one thing that they have in common is the constant growth of their front teeth throughout their lifetime. Depending on the species, rodents can be pets, construction workers, and despised vermin. They are everywhere and have adapted to the urban landscape from their rural roots.

This section will talk about the corporate rodents. They are also all around us doing unseen work, being kept as pets, and carrying devastating disease in our corporate workplace. Start visualizing who these individuals might be as we talk about them in this chapter.

Rats

Rats are viewed as disgusting, disease carrying vermin that infest our cities. They are also viewed as the first ones to leave a sinking ship or flee during a disaster. Rats are very social and have been known to help each other out of captivity situations. They are highly adaptable. They have a reputation as disease carriers and are traditionally known as the culprits behind the Bubonic Plague that killed millions in Europe during the Middle Ages. Rats have also been used to test drugs and cures for disease when the risk to humans was too great. Rats have also been known to be able to predict the sinking of a ship and leave before the imminent danger overtook them.

So much real and symbolic baggage has been associated with the rat that there is probably no one corporate citizen that is that despicable and still working in your organization. Then again, I could be wrong. Let's look at the elements of rat-like corporate behavior and see if we can match them up with individuals that you recognize.

The social interaction of rats is evident in organizations where workers that are seemingly trapped in a situation work together to free each other. This is classic team behavior and is not negative. Altruism among team members is a desirable situation to foster in an organization and is one of the positives among the rat community, at least for the rats.

The adaptability of rats is legendary. They exist naturally in the wild, but have come to easily settle into urban infrastructure to the point where they may outnumber people in some urban areas. Workers in an organization that are adaptable are also desirable making this rat-like quality another desirable trait.

Now for the negative. Let's look at the disease-carrying aspects of our ratty corporate citizens. Negativity can be a disease that will bring an organization to its knees. Negativity can be contagious and can fester into a self-fulfilling prophecy where the worst can come true just because enough people it to be true. It's the power of suggestion and a negative suggestion that runs rampant can bring down a company. The best way to combat negativity is to not perpetuate it. If you avoid it, the contagious effect will not bring you down.

There is the famous notion of rats leaving a sinking ship. This can be very telling in corporate behavior. Turnover in an organization is normal. In work that I've done in healthcare, for example, turnover among nurses is extremely high. There is turnover that is natural among certain positions or within certain industries. There is also turnover that can be telling for the health of an organization. Occasionally organizations will cut a certain percentage of budgets across the board which will result in layoffs or downsizing in multiple areas. What is more of an indicator of an organization's health is a focused turnover in one or two departments. For instance, if a number of resources from the financial and legal department begin to leave an organization, it could signal a negative event that will be forthcoming that could put the organization in financial and legal trouble. Technology resources leaving an organization in groups could signal impending outsourcing of information technology functions. It's important to look at these trends and keep your eyes and ears open if turnover begins to spike in your organization.

Rabbits

Picture cute little fluffy bunnies. They are the cute and cuddly representatives of the rodent community. Yes, they are still rodents. They are one of the more timid, easily preyed upon animals. They rarely bite, even when cornered. They have bones that are easily breakable. Due to their disposition and relatively low maintenance, they make good pets if you are looking for a pet that doesn't interact much other than cuddling and looking cute. Rabbits have a reputation for multiplying uncontrollably, which likely offsets their status as easy prey.

Do we have cute, fluffy bunnies in the corporate world? We do. These are the loyal employees that show up every day. They are taken for granted. Work is heaped on them until they crack. They will not bite back, but will continue to toil away until they collapse. The advice here is not to become a fluffy bunny in your workplace and, if you know one, give him or her a carrot once in a while to show that you care.

Beavers

Busy as a beaver. We've all heard that phrase. Beavers are indeed among the most industrious of animals. They are known for creating dams. When humans create dams, they do it to divert water for construction and to generate power. Beavers do it to form a barricade against predators and to direct food and more building materials to their habitat. They have been known to materially affect the land around them. They live in lodges that safely house their families. The lodges have underwater entrances that don't allow other animals inside.

Corporations can have little pockets of beaver like workers as well. My experience with them is mostly within the realm of information technology (IT). Equipment is ordered and can be diverted through IT for 'testing' and then never be seen again. In small shops, there may be little in the form of checks and balances to prevent this from happening. Because of the IT expertise in one focal area and the lack of expertise in other departments, the underwater entrances into what is being done can be crafted in the form of techno-speak and other technological barriers. In this instance, if you're fortunate to be one of the beavers, keep your eyes and ears open for trouble. If you are not a beaver and you can't swim in the technology current, you may be out of luck.

Chapter 6

Reptiles

Older than man. Stealthily quiet. No natural predator. Rows of razor sharp teeth. Willing to hold onto its victim in an underwater death dance. Corporate attorney? Not quite, it's the crocodile. These fearsome creatures have been known to take down much larger predators once they lure them into their watery habitat. Once those jaws lock onto its prey, there is little hope for survival without traumatic injury.

The crocodile has gone virtually unchanged in millions of years. On land, it is not as fearsome as it is in its natural environment. It's jaws, however, have the strongest bite of any animal when latched on in a bone-crushing, flesh-severing grasp. They can replace each of their 80 teeth more than 50 times during their life span.

Who can you think of in the corporate environment that has been around for a long time and has an unforgiving grasp once prey is caught? Compliance departments come to mind. Corporate compliance has been around since the beginning of corporations, and maybe even before. As long as there are laws governing business, there have been individuals and departments dedicated to enforcing those laws, even when they haven't been broken.

An example from my own professional life comes to mind here. A former employer's corporate compliance officer and corporate counsel was the same person. Think of a shark/crocodile hybrid. Very scary. The company was requiring on-line compliance courses for sexual harassment, hiring practices, and other fun topics. The compliance department took it upon itself to select and administer its own software for delivering these courses. Why use technology experts that are in-house, when you can wing it on your own.

The courses were famous for freezing up or just ending in the middle without warning. One of my employees took one of the courses. He took the exam at the end and passed and it even gave him his score. The mechanism that alerted the compliance department that the course had been completed was not set up correctly. Even though this employee printed the screen showing his score, I was disciplined, as his manager, for him not completing the course. The compliance department would not let this go. It was the only time in my career that I have been disciplined for something.

Rather than join the corporate compliance officer in his death spiral of bureaucracy, I just gave in and escaped his jaws while he was looking the other way. You see, one of his employees had the same issue and he enlisted my department to help uncover the problem even though we had not selected or installed the product. Being the good corporate citizen, we helped. Of course, like any shifty prey, there was an exchange. If he would expunge my disciplinary action for the non-compliance of my employee, I would make sure that no one would find out that a compliance department employee was not in compliance.

Snakes

Snakes; why did it have to be snakes? Often the worst nightmare of the hiker, or anyone for that matter. Why don't we like snakes? Well, those that are poisonous are a bit scary. They can strike with lightning quickness and inject us with toxins that can kill us or make us lose body parts.

The interesting thing about snakes is that most of them are non-venomous. Many of them serve useful purposes like getting rid of rats and other unwanted vermin.

Why do we feel that they are to be avoided? Is it the way they feel, all slimy and scaly? Is it their stealth movement across the ground which gives them the ability to sneak up on us and strike unannounced? Is it their ability to strike quickly and accurately with little warning? It's a combination of all of these.

When we used to watch Steve Irwin, the Crocodile Hunter, sneak up on a deadly snake and pick it up and call it a "beauty", part of us wanted to be able to handle snakes without apparent fear like he did. The other part of us couldn't bear to watch because of the fear that the snake would latch on to him. Despite his apparent recklessness, Irwin had a healthy knowledge and respect for snakes in the wild. We should respect them in the corporate world as well.

When one looks at snakes, there are those that take down their prey with venom, those that squeeze the life out of their prey, and those that swallow their prey whole. Now, the question is who in the corporate jungle conforms to these categories of snakes?

Every company has those that like to spew venom. These are the gossip mongering, passive-aggressive employees that spread their poison at the proverbial water cooler. They strike quickly, and sometimes fatally, with career and reputation damaging rumors and then retreat back into the shadows waiting for their venom to take effect.

There are also corporate snakes that can encircle and employee and squeeze the life out of them. These corporate serpents will identify those employees that can nourish their career and use them for everything they're worth. It might be a technical or clerical resource, but, make no mistakes, these corporate constrictors are squeezing every beneficial ounce of ability out of these designated employees in order to maximize the benefit they can gain, and then will cast aside their used up carcasses when they are no longer useful.

The constrictors are not totally different from the swallowers. When one is being constricted, however, there is still a chance, however small, of escaping likely death. When one is swallowed whole, however, the chance of emerging in the sunlight alive is very small. This difference may not seem significant, but if you are the prey captured by one of these corporate snakes, it is important to remember this difference. It could determine your survival in the organization.

Adaptors

Being able to adapt and blend in to one's background can be a valuable defense mechanism. This is certainly true in the wild if you are trying to avoid becoming prey. It is also an important talent to be able to blend into the background in the corporate world. In nature, we think of the chameleon as having the ultimate talent to blend with its background and avoid being eaten. In the wild, chameleons have specialized cells that allow them to change the pigment in their skin to blend in with their surroundings making them virtually invisible and allowing them to live another day.

The ability to blend in and become invisible within a corporate entity can be valuable as well. At certain times in the corporate lifecycle, it is better to not be noticed. These times include periods of downsizing, staffing for undesirable projects or assignments, and transfers to undesirable areas. Rather than sticking out and being noticed, it is better to blend into the background and be passed over in these situations.

Chapter 7

Amphibians

Amphibians are an interesting class of animal. They usually start out in water as a lesser form of life like a tadpole or larva. They then go through a metamorphosis and develop a respiratory system that is comfortable on land or in the water. They may migrate to the land, but do not lose the ability to go back into the environment they came from.

In the corporate world, the amphibians usually come from the technical areas. That hotshot developer that moved up into management can be a valuable asset. When a project is going off the rails, a technical leader that can relate to the complex tasks many layers down into the project can help the developers rally and bring the project back on track. Of course, the danger with this situation is when that technical manager was a great developer and was promoted into management as a reward for great performance without the skill set or acumen to be a good manager. This fish-out-of-water scenario is all too common. Instead of increasing a resources status in the technical realm, it is assumed that the next logical step is to promote that resource to manager instead of recognizing and rewarding their technical prowess.

Chapter 8

Insects

Myth tells us that when the inevitable apocalypse comes, the cockroaches will crawl from the smoking debris and be the only survivors. If you've ever tried to squash one of these insects, you've discovered their near indestructability. Cockroaches have been known to survive for weeks without food or water. They've been known to survive by eating wallpaper glue. Roaches can live a substantially long time even when their heads have been removed.

Who do you know in your corporate world that has characteristics like this? Think about those people that survive mergers, acquisitions, audits, and other events that affect the organization. Usually they have chameleon-like attributes (see the section on adaptors). They become part of the fabric of a company. CEOs come and go, yet these individuals survive.

Chapter 9

Hidden in the Deep

We're gonna need a bigger boat. Sharks. They strike fear in the hearts of swimmers. They have evolved into the perfect predatory machine. They must keep moving to survive and basically eat everything in their path. It's no mystery where I'm going in equating the shark with its equivalent in the corporate world. Sharks and lawyers have been equated since the first lawyer passed the bar. In my experience, the high level of ruthlessness exhibited by the scariest predator in the known universe cannot be compared in this way. Sharks are as docile as a bag of puppies compared to corporate lawyers on the prowl.

Chapter 10

The Prey

The Fast and the Furious

Most of us in the corporate world are prey. In the jungle, prey provides the fuel that keeps the rest of the fuel chain surviving from day to day. In the corporate world, prey are those people that have their knowledge, skills, and abilities fed on by leadership day after day so that the corporate food chain can stay nourished. Is it bad to be prey in the corporate jungle? It depends. If you are completely devoured and used up by the predators, your usefulness can be impacted. If you can limit the predators to "small bites" by having a clever defense mechanism, you just might survive in a way that all parties can benefit.

The Fast

One way that prey can survive the advances of predators is through the use of speed. Speed as a defense mechanism can be useful. Like the old joke about the bear in the woods, to survive, you don't have to outrun the bear; you only have to outrun the other people you are with. There are many animals that are considered prey that run very fast.

The Wildebeest

For anyone that saw The Lion King, you will remember the thunderous stampede of wildebeest that brought about the demise of Simba's father. At 500 pounds and the capability to run 50 miles per hour, the wildebeest, which runs in herds, can be a formidable animal for a predator to take down. It's usually the slow, sick, and elderly that fall victim to predators. Since their average lifespan is about 20 years, they must outrun a number of predators before age or sickness slows them down. The wildebeest has the unique ability to recognize danger, not only from their own herd, but through interpretation of the danger alarms from other prey.

Who are the wildebeest in the corporate jungle? Well, they carry a lot of weight and have usually been around for a while. They can sense danger in their own functional area, or through the events taking place in others. They can outrun and outlast executives and management that seek to prey on their knowledge and experience. Finally, after many years of running, they just tire out and give up the ghost. Hopefully this is through retirement or finding a new job and not literally checking out. Look for people in technology, finance, and other departments where knowledge is king to find your corporate wildebeest herd.

The Springbok

The springbok is also a very fast animal. It has speed in common with the wildebeest. In fact, it's slightly faster, clocking in at 56 miles per hour. What it doesn't have in common is size and longevity. Springbok weigh in at 80-110 pounds and they only live for about 7-9 years. They are extremely agile. They have the unique trait that allows them to survive without drinking water. They get all of the moisture they need from the plants that they eat. This means that they never have their head down or their attention drawn from sensing danger.

The corporate springbok is an interesting form of prey. I would put individuals in this category that are extremely agile and can move quickly through tasks without much care and feeding. The fact is, at this stage in their career, they are lightweights. They are usually bright-eyed recent college graduates that might be working for an organization to gain knowledge and training. They stay around long enough to get what they need and then move to another organization. Sometimes the move puts them higher on the food chain until they reach their ultimate potential. Watch out for those springboks. Today's springbok might end up being tomorrow's predator.

Beware of the Fastest Land Animal

Wildebeest may be big and somewhat fast. Springboks are small, agile and quite speedy. These four legged prey at nearly 60 miles per hour are no match for the cheetah which clocks in at 70 miles per hour. They can keep up this pace for a full 8-10 minutes. What this tells us is that even the fastest of the animals that are considered prey cannot avoid the fastest predator. This is true in the corporate world. Remember, you don't have to outrun the predator; you just have to outrun the slowest of the other prey.

What Does it all Mean?

This book was an attempt to introduce you to my view on the corporate world. It is the first of many that I will release based on my many years in corporate America. I use humor to equate corporate personality types to creatures in the wild, but there is a degree of truth that permeates throughout the book. I hope that you've enjoyed it and will spread the word.

About the Author

Scott Rancor had spent a number of years in corporate America as an executive and a consultant. He has seen it all and has decided to write about it. He currently resides in Boston, MA.

www.ingramcontent.com/pod-product-compliance
Lightning Source LLC
Chambersburg PA
CBHW051253170526
45165CB00004B/1691